The Thirteen Colonies

Kate Connell

PICTURE CREDITS

Cover © Michael Schwarz/The Image Works; pages 2-3, 34-b © Giraudon/Art Resource; pages 6-7, 26 (top and bottom), 31 (left bottom) © Bettmann/Corbis; pages 10 (bottom), 11 (bottom), 13 (bottom), 25 (left and right bottom), 28 (top), 29 (bottom), 30 (left middle and bottom), 31 (right middle), 34-d and e, 35-b © The Granger Collection, New York; pages 8 (bottom), 31 (right top), 34-a © APVA Preservation Virginia; 9 (bottom), 12(bottom), 25 (right top), 30 (right middle & bottom), 34-c, 35-a © Hulton Archive/Getty Images; page 14 © Museum of the City of New York; pages 16-17 © Joseph Sohm; Visions of America/Corbis; pages 18 (top), 19 (bottom), 22 (right middle), 23 (bottom), 31 (left middle) © Ted Curtin/Plimoth Plantation; page 20 (top) © Michael Schwarz; pages 21 (bottom), 22 (top) © Sisse Brimberg/National Geographic Society; page 26 (bottom) © David G. Houser/Corbis; page 28 (bottom) © Brand X Pictures/Getty Images; page 30 (right bottom) © Corbis; page 32 © Lee Snider/Photo Images/Corbis; page 36 Catherine Karnow/Corbis

Produced through the worldwide resources of the National Geographic Society, John M. Fahey, Jr., President and Chief Executive Officer; Gilbert M. Grosvenor, Chairman of the Board; Nina D. Hoffman, Executive Vice President and President, Books and Education Publishing Group.

PREPARED BY NATIONAL GEOGRAPHIC SCHOOL PUBLISHING

Ericka Markman, Senior Vice President and President, Children's Books and Education Publishing Group; Steve Mico, Senior Vice President, Editorial Director, Publisher; Francis Downey, Executive Editor; Richard Easby, Editorial Manager; Anne Stone, Lori Dibble Collins, Editors; Bea Jackson, Director of Layout and Design; Jim Hiscott, Design Manager; Cynthia Olson, Art Director; Margaret Sidlosky, Illustrations Director; Matt Wascavage, Manager of Publishing Services; Sean Philpotts, Jane Ponton, Production Managers; Ted Tucker, Production Specialist.

MANUFACTURING AND QUALITY CONTROL

Christopher A. Liedel, Chief Financial Officer; Phillip L. Schlosser, Director; Clifton M. Brown III, Manager

CONSULTANT AND REVIEWER

J.M. Opal, Colby College

BOOK DESIGN/PHOTO RESEARCH

Steve Curtis Design, Inc.

◄ Colonists and Native Americans made peace treaties.

Contents

Copyright © 2006 National Geographic Society.
All Rights Reserved. Reproduction of the whole or any part of the
contents without written permission from the publisher is prohibited.
National Geographic, National Geographic School Publishing,
National Geographic Reading Expeditions, and the Yellow Border
are registered trademarks of the National Geographic Society.

Published by the National Geographic Society
1145 17th Street N.W.
Washington, D.C. 20036-4688

ISBN: 0-7922-5453-8

2010　2009　2008
　　4 5 6 7 8 9 10 11 12 13 14 15

Printed in Canada.

Building Colonies

North
America

Colonies

Atlantic Ocean

In 1492, Europeans started exploring North America. This land was a new world to them. Europeans soon began to move there. Many of them came from England. They built small towns. These were the first English **colonies** in North America. A colony is a place ruled by another country.

colony – a place ruled by another country

▼ Ships carried people from England to build colonies in North America.

England

Europe

Moving

Big Idea

People moved to the 13 colonies for different reasons.

Set Purpose

Read to learn about the colonies.

▼ Pilgrims landed at Plymouth, Massachusetts, in 1620.

Where were the 13 colonies located?

Why did people settle in the colonies?

to America

Europeans began moving to North America in the late 1500s. The trip was long and dangerous. Most people knew that they would never see family and friends again. So why did they move?

Europeans moved to North America for different reasons. Some came to earn money or to own land. Others came for religious reasons.

Moving for a Better Life

England **founded** its first lasting colony in North America in 1607. The colony was named Jamestown. It is in Virginia.

The people who lived in Jamestown were called **colonists.** Many of the colonists in Jamestown moved there to make money. Some grew **crops** that could be sold. Most came as servants. They had to work for someone else.

....

found – to start or set up
colonist – a person who lives in a colony
crop – a plant that is grown to be used

▼ Jamestown started out as a small colony.

Looking for a Cash Crop

At first, life in Jamestown was very hard. The colonists had little food to eat. They often fought with the Native Americans who already lived in the area. Many colonists died.

Despite the **hardships,** more colonists moved to Jamestown. Life started getting better for them around 1619. That is when they found a way to make money. They grew tobacco. They sold this crop to England.

....
hardship – a problem

▼ Colonists grew tobacco to sell to England.

Other Colonies Founded

Jamestown was not the only colony. Colonists also moved to other areas of North America. In 1620, a small group of people founded Plymouth Colony in Massachusetts. These colonists were known as **Pilgrims.**

Plymouth was the second lasting English colony in North America. Soon there would be many more.

....

Pilgrim – a person who helped found Plymouth Colony

▼ Pilgrims began to build their new colony.

10

Moving for Religious Reasons

Most of the Pilgrims moved for religious reasons. They wanted to be free to practice their own religion.

In England, the government told people what religion they had to believe in. People who had different beliefs were called **dissenters.** The Pilgrims were one group of dissenters. Some other groups of dissenters founded other colonies.

....
dissenter – a person who has different religious beliefs

▼ **Pilgrims practiced their religion at church.**

Work in the Colonies

As the colonies grew, the colonists needed to find more workers. Many workers were **indentured servants.** These were people who agreed to work if someone paid for their trip to America.

Most indentured servants worked for five to seven years to pay off their debt. They could not choose where they lived or who they worked for. Near Jamestown, more than seven of every ten colonists were indentured servants!

indentured servant – a person who worked to pay for the trip to America

▼ These indentured servants worked at loading a ship.

Enslaved Africans

Some colonists had **slaves** do their work. Colonists bought thousands of slaves. The slaves had been captured in Africa and brought to North America.

Slaves worked on farms and in cities. They did all kinds of work. They made a lot of money for their owners. Slaves could not choose who they worked for or where they lived. Most never earned their freedom. Slavery was allowed in all of England's colonies in North America.

slave – a person who is forced to work without pay

▼ Slaves tended the tobacco crop.

The Thirteen Colonies

Over time, more people came to America. The colonists needed more room. They began to found other colonies. Colonists founded colonies in Rhode Island, Connecticut, New York, Pennsylvania, and elsewhere.

By 1733, England had 13 colonies in North America. All the colonies were close to the Atlantic Ocean. They stretched from Massachusetts to Georgia.

Everyone who came to the colonies helped build America. Free people, indentured servants, and slaves helped make America the country it is today.

▼ Small towns grew into larger cities as more colonists settled in America.

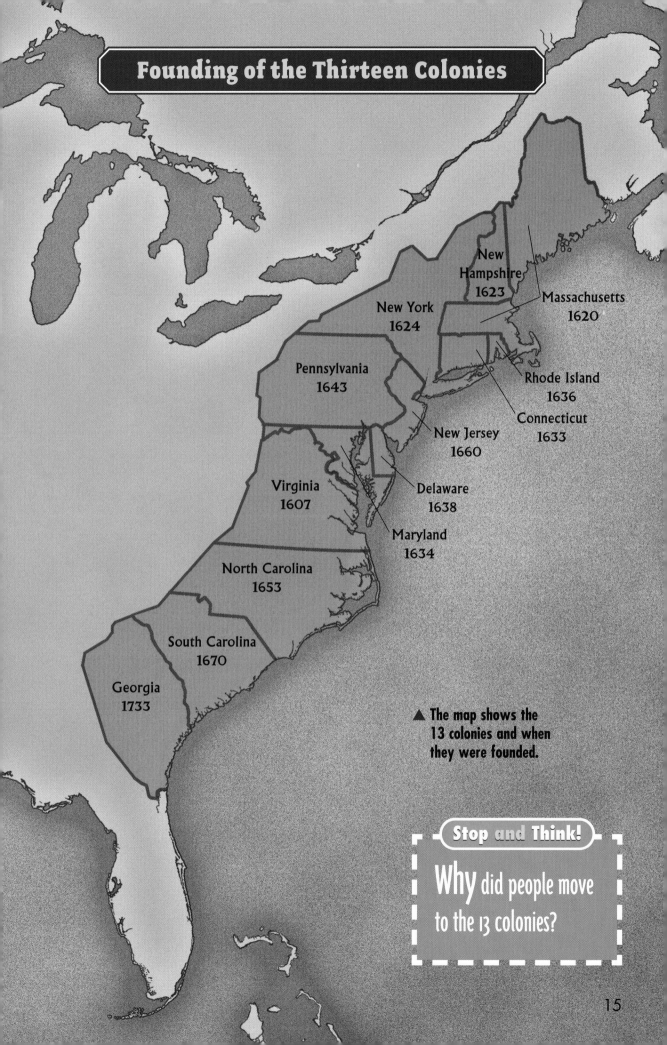

Founding of the Thirteen Colonies

New Hampshire 1623

Massachusetts 1620

New York 1624

Rhode Island 1636

Connecticut 1633

Pennsylvania 1643

New Jersey 1660

Virginia 1607

Delaware 1638

Maryland 1634

North Carolina 1653

South Carolina 1670

Georgia 1733

▲ The map shows the 13 colonies and when they were founded.

Stop and Think!

Why did people move to the 13 colonies?

Setting Sail for Plymouth

Recap
Explain why people moved to the colonies.

Set Purpose
Now explore what life was like for the colonists.

▶ Pilgrims sailed to America on the *Mayflower.*

Colony

On September 6, 1620, a crew of sailors and 102 passengers set sail for America. Their ship was called the *Mayflower*. The passengers came to be known as Pilgrims. Most of them were looking for religious freedom.

Their journey was long and dangerous. It lasted more than two months. Finally the Pilgrims saw land. They called their new home Plymouth Colony.

▲ The Pilgrims built a fence like this around their houses for protection.

Building a Colony

When the Pilgrims arrived in America, they had no houses to live in. They lived aboard the *Mayflower* for many months. During the day, they left the ship to build their houses. At night, they returned to the ship to sleep.

By late spring, the Pilgrims had built enough houses for everyone. They had also built a fence to protect their houses. At last, the *Mayflower* returned to England. The Pilgrims stayed behind. Plymouth Colony was now their home.

Making a Home

Most Pilgrim houses were small and plain. They had dirt floors. Most houses had a fireplace and one main room. Some also had a tiny room upstairs.

Many Pilgrims had a garden. They had to grow some of their own food. They planted beans, cabbage, and carrots in the spring. They also planted spinach and squash. These crops helped feed people all year long.

▼ **The Pilgrims grew some of their food in gardens like this one.**

Fireplace

▲ Pilgrim women cooked over an open fire like this one.

A Simple Life

Pilgrims used fireplaces to heat their homes and to provide some light. Fireplaces were also used for cooking. Women cooked in big pots that hung over the fire.

The Pilgrims did not have many belongings. They brought only a few things with them on the *Mayflower*. Most families had a chair or two, some pots, and a few tools.

Work, Work, Work

Life was not easy for the Pilgrims. They had to work very hard. Their houses did not have running water. People gathered water from streams and carried it home.

Everyone had chores, even children. Girls helped with sewing and washing clothes. Boys helped tend the goats and pigs. Each person had a job to do.

▼ Pilgrims used buckets to carry water home from the stream.

▲ Pilgrims hunted ducks and planted corn to survive.

Learning to Survive

The Pilgrims needed help. They made friends with some of the Native Americans who lived nearby. The Native Americans taught the Pilgrims how to grow corn. They showed the Pilgrims about life in their new land.

Slowly the Pilgrims learned how to survive. They hunted ducks and other wild animals for food. They caught fish and gathered wild berries. They also planted crops such as corn.

Giving Thanks

The Pilgrims celebrated their first **harvest** in the fall. They shared a meal with their Native American friends. They also played games. The harvest celebration lasted three days. People had many reasons to be thankful.

Today, when we celebrate Thanksgiving, we remember the Pilgrims of Plymouth Colony. We also remember the Native Americans who helped them survive in their new home.

harvest – the gathering of crops

▼ **The Pilgrims held a feast like this one to celebrate their first harvest.**

Stop and Think!

What was life like for the Pilgrims?

Recap

Explain what life was like for the Pilgrims of Plymouth Colony.

Set Purpose

Now learn more about the 13 colonies.

CONNECT WHAT YOU HAVE LEARNED

The Thirteen Colonies

Europeans began moving to North America in the late 1500s. They built small towns called colonies. Over time the colonies grew.

Here are some ideas that you learned about the 13 colonies.

- England had 13 colonies in what is now the United States.
- Some colonists came to America to make money.
- Some colonists came to America so that they could practice their religion.
- Indentured servants and slaves did much of the work in the colonies.

Check What You Have Learned

Why did people move to the colonies?

▲ All 13 colonies were near the Atlantic Ocean.

▲ Colonists in Virginia made money by selling tobacco.

▲ Pilgrims moved to America for religious reasons.

▲ Slavery was allowed in all 13 colonies.

The Other Colonies

Several European countries founded colonies in North America. England had 13 colonies along the coast of the Atlantic Ocean. France owned colonies north and west of the 13 colonies. Spain had colonies to the south. Colonists from these different areas often fought one another.

▼ **Spanish colonists built this fort in Florida.**

▲ The Vikings may have been the first Europeans to see America.

The Discoverers

Many people think Columbus discovered America. But he was not the first European ever to see America. In about 1000, Vikings explored parts of North America. The Vikings did not build permanent colonies. Their trips were soon forgotten.

◀ A Viking in battle armor

Spreading the News

Some colonists wrote letters to one another. But getting a letter from one colony to another was not easy. There was no mail service.

A letter writer often handed a letter to a traveler. That person would pass the letter along to another traveler. Eventually, the letter would get to the right person.

Each person who carried a letter would read it. These people were not nosy. They just wanted to read the latest news. There were no newspapers. Letter writers expected others to read their mail.

▲ Colonists used feather quills and ink to write.

A Witch Scare

One of the most amazing events in the 13 colonies happened in 1692. That is when 9-year-old Betty Parris and her cousin Abigail Williams fell ill. The two girls lived in Salem Village, Massachusetts.

Some people thought witches had caused the girls to fall sick. Most people believed in witches at the time. Witchcraft was a crime. People panicked. By the end of the year, 144 people had been arrested for witchcraft. When it was over, more than 20 people had been put to death for witchcraft.

▼ **This woman was put on trial for witchcraft in Salem Village.**

Many kinds of words are used in this book. Here you will learn about nouns. You will also learn about proper nouns.

Nouns

A noun is a word that names a person, place, or thing. Use the nouns below in your own sentences.

England founded its first **colony** in North America in 1607.

The colonists in Jamestown grew **tobacco.**

The Pilgrims were **dissenters.**

Most indentured **servants** worked for five to seven years.

Proper Nouns

A proper noun is a word that names a specific person, place, or thing. Proper nouns always begin with a capital letter. Can you find all the proper nouns in the sentences below?

Europeans began moving to **North America** in the 1500s.

The first lasting English colony was **Jamestown.**

Plymouth Colony was in **Massachusetts.**

The **Pilgrims** moved to Plymouth for religious reasons.

The Pilgrims sailed to America on the **Mayflower.**

All the colonies were close to the **Atlantic Ocean.**

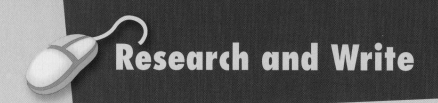

Research and Write

Write About Colonial America

Learn more about the colonies. Choose one of the 13 colonies and find out why people settled there. What was life like in the colony? Who was the leader of the colony?

Research
Collect books and reference materials, or go online.

Read and Take Notes
As you read, take notes and draw pictures.

Write
Draw a picture of the colony that you chose. Write a paragraph describing your picture.

▶ **William Penn founded the Pennsylvania colony.**

Read and Compare

Read More About Colonial America

Find and read other books about America during colonial times. As you read, think about these questions.

- Why did people move to the colonies?
- How were the 13 colonies alike and how were they different?
- How was colonial life different from life today?

Books to Read

▲ Read about the settlement of the Jamestown colony.

▲ Travel with the Pilgrims as they set sail from England to North America.

▲ Learn more about the adventures of a boy in colonial America.

Glossary

KEY CONCEPT

colonist (page 8)

A person who lives in a colony

The colonists tried to make better lives in America.

KEY CONCEPT

colony (page 5)

A place ruled by another country

The English founded a colony called Jamestown.

crop (page 8)

A plant that is grown to be used

Colonists wanted to grow crops that they could sell to England.

dissenter (page 11)

A person who has different religious beliefs

The Pilgrims were dissenters.

KEY CONCEPT

found (page 8)

To start or set up

England founded its first lasting colony in North America in 1607.

hardship (page 9)
A problem
The colonists faced many hardships.

harvest (page 23)
The gathering of crops
The Pilgrims celebrated their first harvest with a feast.

indentured servant (page 12)
A person who worked to pay for the trip to America
Most indentured servants worked for five to seven years.

Pilgrim (page 10)
A person who helped found Plymouth Colony
The Pilgrims started building their colony in 1620.

slave (page 13)
A person who is forced to work without pay
Some colonists had slaves to do their work.

Index